THE LITTLE BOOK OF
POSITIVE
QUOTATIONS

THE LITTLE BOOK OF
POSITIVE
QUOTATIONS

Compiled and Arranged
by Steve Deger and Leslie Ann Gibson

Fairview Press
Minneapolis

Published by Fairview Press, 2450 Riverside Avenue, Minneapolis, MN 55454. For a free current catalog of Fairview Press titles, call toll-free 1-800-544-8207, or visit our Web site at www.fairviewpress.org.

Fairview Press is a division of Fairview Health Services, a community-focused health system, affiliated with the University of Minnesota, providing a complete range of services, from the prevention of illness and injury to care for the most complex medical conditions.

Library of Congress Cataloging-in-Publication Data
The little book of positive quotations / compiled and arranged by Steve Deger and Leslie Ann Gibson.
    p. cm.
ISBN-13: 978-1-57749-158-3 (pbk. : alk. paper)
ISBN-10: 1-57749-158-0 (pbk. : alk. paper)
1. Success—Quotations, maxims, etc. 2. Conduct of life—Quotations, maxims, etc. I. Deger, Steve, 1966- II. Gibson, Leslie Ann, 1956-
PN6084.S78L58 2006
646.7—dc22

                                        2006016567

Printed in Canada
First printing: October 2006
10 09 08 07   7 6 5 4 3

Cover design: Laurie Ingram

For our nephews and nieces,
most of whom aren't so "little" anymore!

Chad Baucom, Randy Baucom,
Andrea Burnham, Aaron Burnham,
Chris Lungstrom, Eric Gibson, Evan Gibson,
Sarah Gibson, Alex Hill, Hannah Hill,
Sam Hill, Danny Strapple, and Niki Strapple

CONTENTS

WELCOMING JOY INTO YOUR LIFE

JOY AND LOVE IMPROVE
ALL ASPECTS OF LIFE

She was one of those happily created beings who please without effort, make friends everywhere, and take life so gracefully and easily that less fortunate souls are tempted to believe that such are born under a lucky star.

—Louisa May Alcott

Love conquers all things.

—Virgil

The general rule is that people who enjoy life also enjoy marriage.

—Phyllis Battelle

Love, and do what you like.

—St. Augustine

Cheerfulness keeps up a kind of daylight in the mind, and fills it with a steady and perpetual serenity.

—Joseph Addison

I went back to being an amateur, in the sense of somebody who loves what she is doing. If a professional loses the love of work, routine sets in, and that's the death of work and life.

—Ada Bethune

Where there is laughter there is always more health than sickness.

—Phyllis Bottome

There is no cosmetic for beauty like happiness.

—Lady Marguerite Blessington

No man is a failure who is enjoying life.

—William Feather

Happiness is when what you think, what you say, and what you do are in harmony.

—Mahatma Gandhi

The joyfulness of a man prolongeth his days.

—Ecclesiasticus

The Time to Be Happy Is Now

There is no cure for birth and death, save to
enjoy the interval.

—George Santayana

For years I wanted to be older, and now I am.

—Margaret Atwood

You have to do what you love to do, not get
stuck in that comfort zone of a regular job.
Life is not a dress rehearsal. This is it.

—Lucinda Basset

The best way to secure future happiness is to
be as happy as is rightfully possible today.

—Charles W. Eliot

Death twitches my ear. "Live," he says; "I
am coming."

—Virgil

Our faith in the present dies out long
before our faith in the future.

—Ruth Benedict

Old and young, we are all on our last cruise.
—Robert Louis Stevenson

The idea came to me that I was, am, and will be, but perhaps will not become. This did not scare me. There was for me in being an intensity I did not feel in becoming.
—Nina Berberova

Forget the past and live the present hour.
—Sarah Knowles Bolton

Paradise is here or nowhere: you must take your joy with you or you will never find it.
—O. S. Marden

Only when your consciousness is totally focused on the moment you are in can you receive whatever gift, lesson, or delight that moment has to offer.
—Barbara de Angelis

The best part of our lives we pass in counting on what is to come.
—William Hazlitt

WE CAN SUMMON JOY
EVEN IN TIMES OF HARDSHIP

The art of life is to know how to enjoy a
little and to endure very much.
—William Hazlitt

I like living. I have sometimes been wildly,
despairingly, acutely miserable, racked with
sorrow, but through it all I still know quite
certainly that just to be alive is a grand thing.
—Agatha Christie

Think of all the beauty that's still left in and
around you and be happy!
—Anne Frank

Your joy is your sorrow unmasked. And the
selfsame well from which your laughter rises
was oftentimes filled with your tears.
—Kahlil Gibran

Joy is more divine than sorrow, for joy is
bread and sorrow is medicine.
—Henry Ward Beecher

The sweetest joy, the wildest woe, is love.
—Pearl Bailey

Hope costs nothing.

—Colette

Love is like a beautiful flower which I may not touch, but whose fragrance makes the garden a place of delight just the same.
—Helen Keller

Hope is the last thing to abandon the unhappy.
—Anon.

Weeping may endure for a night, but joy cometh in the morning.
—Psalms 30:5

So they speak soothingly about progress and the greatest possible happiness, forgetting that happiness is itself poisoned if the measure of suffering has not been fulfilled.
—Carl Jung

WE SHOULDN'T RELY ON EXTERNAL THINGS FOR HAPPINESS

Happiness is found in doing, not merely possessing.

—Napoleon Hill

I don't sit around thinking that I'd like to have another husband; only another man would make me think that way.

—Lauren Bacall

Happiness is a conscious choice, not an automatic response.

—Mildred Barthel

There is only one way to happiness, and that is to cease worrying about things which are beyond the power of our will.

—Epictetus

My life has no purpose, no direction, no aim, no meaning, and yet I'm happy. I can't figure it out. What am I doing right?

—Charles Schulz

Our concern must be to live while we're
alive … to release our inner selves from the
spiritual death that comes with living
behind a facade designed to conform to
external definitions of who and what we are.
                              —Elisabeth Kübler-Ross

Joy is not in things, it is in us.
                              —Benjamin Franklin

Seek not outside yourself, heaven is within.
                              —Mary Lou Cook

It is neither wealth nor splendor, but
tranquility and occupation, which give
happiness.
                              —Thomas Jefferson

Joy has nothing to do with material things,
or with a man's outward circumstance … a
man living in the lap of luxury can be
wretched, and a man in the depths of
poverty can overflow with joy.
                              —William Barclay

IF WE ARE OPEN TO JOY, IT WILL REVEAL ITSELF

When I first open my eyes upon the morning meadows and look out upon the beautiful world, I thank God I am alive.
—Ralph Waldo Emerson

We hear voices in solitude, we never hear in the hurry and turmoil of life; we receive counsels and comforts we get under no other condition.
—Amelia Barr

The path to cheerfulness is to sit cheerfully and to act and speak as if cheerfulness were already there.
—William James

Everything holds its breath except spring. She bursts through as strong as ever.
—B. M. Bower

Loving is half of believing.
—Victor Hugo

Life has no other discipline to impose, if we would but realize it, than to accept life unquestioningly. Everything we shut our eyes to, everything we run away from, everything we deny, denigrate or despise, serves to defeat us in the end. What seems nasty, painful, evil, can become a source of beauty, joy and strength, if faced with an open mind.

—Henry Miller

Growth itself contains the germ of happiness.

—Pearl S. Buck

Happiness often sneaks in through a door you didn't know you left open.

—John Barrymore

Celebrate the happiness that friends are always giving, make every day a holiday and celebrate just living!

—Amanda Bradley

We are new every day.

—Irene Claremont Castillego

The universe is full of magical things patiently waiting for our wits to grow sharper.
—Eden Phillpotts

What a wonderful life I've had! I only wish I had realized it sooner.
—Colette

Happiness is something that comes into our lives through doors we don't even remember leaving open.
—Rose Wilder Lane

Happiness is to be found along the way, not at the end of the road, for then the journey is over and it is too late.
—Robert R. Updegraff

Today a new sun rises for me; everything lives, everything is animated, everything seems to speak to me of my passion, everything invites me to cherish it.
—Anne Lenclos

MAKE THE MOST OF EVERY MOMENT

Sometimes I would rather have people take away years of my life than take away a moment.

—Pearl Bailey

Men who never get carried away should be.

—Malcolm Forbes

You are younger today than you ever will be again. Make use of it for the sake of tomorrow.

—Anon.

I have always felt that the moment when first you wake up in the morning is the most wonderful of the twenty-four hours. No matter how weary or dreary you may feel, you possess the certainty that … absolutely anything may happen. And the fact that it practically always doesn't, matters not one jot. The possibility is always there.

—Monica Baldwin

SHARE YOUR JOY

Grief can take care of itself, but to get the full value of a joy, you must have somebody to divide it with.

—Mark Twain

Shared joys make a friend, not shared sufferings.

—Friedrich Wilhelm Nietzsche

To be kind to all, to like many and love a few, to be needed and wanted by those we love, is certainly the nearest we can come to happiness.

—Mary Roberts Rinehart

Friendship redoubleth joys, and cutteth griefs in half.

—Francis Bacon

Celebrate the happiness that friends are always giving, make every day a holiday and celebrate just living!

—Amanda Bradley

I learned quickly that when I made others laugh, they liked me.

—Art Buchwald

I felt an earnest and humble desire, and I shall do it till I die, to increase the stock of harmless cheerfulness.

—Charles Dickens

Kindness begets kindness.

—Greek proverb

What sunshine is to flowers, smiles are to humanity. These are but trifles, to be sure; but, scattered along life's pathway, the good they do is inconceivable.

—Joseph Addison

HELPING OTHERS

When We Help, We Show Compassion

One of the most valuable things we can do to heal one another is listen to each other's stories.
—Rebecca Falls

Grant that we may not so much seek to be consoled as to console. To be understood as to understand.
—St. Francis of Assisi

I see their souls, and I hold them in my hands, and because I love them they weigh nothing.
—Pearl Bailey

One's life has value so long as one attributes value to the life of others, by means of love, friendship, indignation, and compassion.
—Simone de Beauvoir

Tenderness is greater proof of love than the most passionate of vows.
—Marlene Dietrich

Sympathy is the charm of human life.
                    —Grace Aguilar

It is not until you become a mother that
your judgment slowly turns to compassion
and understanding.
                    —Erma Bombeck

I'd like people to think of me as someone
who cares about them.
                    —Diana, Princess of Wales

Kindness is loving people more than they
deserve.
                    —Joseph Joubert

Compassion is the antitoxin of the soul.
                    —Eric Hoffer

The individual is capable of both great
compassion and great indifference. He has
it within his means to nourish the former
and outgrow the latter.
                    —Norman Cousins

HELP, BUT DON'T INTRUDE

Don't give advice unless you're asked.
                              —Amy Alcott

Listen long enough and the person will
generally come up with an adequate solution.
                              —Mary Kay Ash

Goodness that preaches undoes itself.
                              —Ralph Waldo Emerson

Never help a child with a task at which he
feels he can succeed.
                              —Maria Montessori

Often we can help each other most by
leaving each other alone; at other times we
need the hand-grasp and the word of cheer.
                              —Elbert Hubbard

Kindness affects more than severity.

                              —Aesop

WE HELP WHEN WE
SET A GOOD EXAMPLE

The essential element in personal magnetism is a consuming sincerity—an overwhelming faith in the importance of the work one has to do.

—Bruce Barton

Strong beliefs win strong men, and then make them stronger.

—Walter Bagehot

This, then, is the test we must set for ourselves; not to march alone but to march in such a way that others will wish to join us.

—Hubert H. Humphrey

A good character is the best tombstone. Those who loved you, and were helped by you, will remember you when forget-me-nots have withered. Carve your name on hearts, not on marble.

—Charles Hadden Spurgeon

We deceive ourselves when we fancy that only weakness needs support. Strength needs it far more.

—Anne-Sophie Swetchine

The hardest job kids face today is learning good manners without seeing any.

—Fred Astaire

Example is the best precept.

—Aesop

What you teach your own children is what you really believe in.

—Cathy Warner Weatherford

Example is the school of mankind, and they will learn at no other.

—Edmund Burke

Example has more followers than reason. We unconsciously imitate what pleases us.

—Christian Nevell Bovee

If you can't be a good example, then you'll just have to be a horrible warning.
—Catherine Aird

Well done is better than well said.
—Benjamin Franklin

Nothing is so contagious as an example. We never do great good or great evil without bringing about more of the same on the part of others.
—François de La Rochefoucauld

Example moves the world more than doctrine. The great exemplars are the poets of action.
—Henry Miller

Example is not the main thing in influencing others. It is the only thing.
—Albert Schwietzer

The road to learning by precept is long, but by example short and effective.
—Seneca

HELPING OTHERS HELPS US GROW

The best way to cheer yourself up is to try
to cheer somebody else.
> —Mark Twain

If you do a good job for others, you heal
yourself at the same time, because a dose of
joy is a spiritual cure.
> —Ed Sullivan

There is nothing to make you like other
human beings so much as doing things for
them.
> —Zora Neale Hurston

In helping others, we shall help ourselves,
for whatever good we give out completes
the circle and comes back to us.
> —Flora Edwards

We challenge one another to be funnier and
smarter.... It's the way friends make love to
one another.
> —Annie Gottlieb

What I spent, is gone; what I kept, I lost;
but what I gave away will be mine forever.
—Ethel Percy Andrus

When someone does something good,
applaud! You will make two people happy.
—Samuel Goldwyn

The comforter's head never aches.
—Italian proverb

Joint undertakings stand a better chance
when they benefit both sides.
—Euripides

The habit of being uniformly considerate
toward others will bring increased happiness
to you.
—Grenville Kleiser

To devote a portion of one's leisure to do
something for someone else is one of the
highest forms of recreation.
—Gerald B. Fitzgerald

LIFE IS ABOUT CARING FOR OTHERS

Friends are an aid to the young, to guard them from error; to the elderly, to attend to their wants and to supplement their failing power of action; to those in the prime of life, to assist them to noble deeds.

—Aristotle

A happy life is made up of little things—a gift sent, a letter written, a call made, a recommendation given, transportation provided, a cake made, a book lent, a check sent.

—Carol Holmes

The legacy I want to leave is a child-care system that says no kid is going to be left alone or left unsafe.

—Marian Wright Edelman

We live very close together. So, our prime purpose in this life is to help others.

—Dalai Lama

The most satisfying thing in life is to have been able to give a large part of one's self to others.
—Pierre Teilhard de Chardin

There are high spots in all of our lives and most of them have come about through encouragement from someone else.
—George M. Adams

We've got to work to save our children and do it with full respect for the fact that if we do not, no one else is going to do it.
—Dorothy Height

Follow your interests, get the best available education and training, set your sights high, be persistent, be flexible, keep your options open, accept help when offered, and be prepared to help others.
—Mildred Spiewak Dresselhaus

Kindness is the golden chain by which society is bound together.
—Johann von Goethe

WE HELP BY TEACHING

The teacher is one who makes two ideas grow where only one grew before.
                              —Elbert Hubbard

If a child is to keep alive his inborn sense of wonder … he needs the companionship of at least one adult who can share it, rediscovering with him the joy, excitement, and mystery of the world we live in.
                              —Rachel Carson

We ought to be doing all we can to make it possible for every child to fulfill his or her God-given potential.
                              —Hillary Rodham Clinton

The greatest good you can do for another is not just to share your riches, but to reveal to him his own.
                              —Benjamin Disraeli

REMEMBER FRIENDS,
NEIGHBORS, AND FAMILY

If a friend is in trouble, don't annoy him by asking if there is anything you can do. Think up something appropriate and do it.
—Edgar Watson Howe

You leave home to seek your fortune and, when you get it, you go home and share it with your family.
—Anita Baker

My heart is happy, my mind is free. I had a father who talked with me.
—Hilde Bigelow

A man is selfish not for pursuing his own good, but for neglecting his neighbor's.
—Richard Whately

Where *our* bread is concerned, it is a material matter. Where our *neighbor's* bread is concerned, it is a spiritual matter.
—I. D. Douglas

BELIEVING IN YOURSELF

Don't Let Others Stand in Your Way

As you go along your road in life, you will,
if you aim high enough, also meet resistance
… but no matter how tough the opposition
may seem, have courage still—and persevere.
—Madeleine Albright

The Wright brothers flew through the
smoke screen of impossibility.
—Dorothea Brande

He that respects himself is safe from others,
he wears a coat of mail that none can pierce.
—Henry Wadsworth Longfellow

There is just one life for each of us: our
own.
—Euripides

Nothing is good for everyone, but only
relatively to some people.
—André Gide

EVERYTHING BEGINS WITH SELF-LOVE

To understand is to forgive, even oneself.
                    —Alexander Chase

To love others, we must first learn to love ourselves.

                    —Anon.

To love oneself is the beginning of a lifelong romance.

                    —Oscar Wilde

Love yourself first and everything else falls into line. You really have to love yourself to get anything done in this world.
                    —Lucille Ball

To be nobody but yourself—in a world which is doing its best, night and day, to make you everybody else—means to fight the hardest battle which any human being can fight, and never stop fighting.
                    —e. e. cummings

OVERCOME YOUR FEARS

From a shy, timid girl I had become a woman of resolute character, who could no longer be frightened by the struggle with troubles.

—Anna Dostoevsky

Jealousy is the fear or apprehension of superiority; envy our uneasiness under it.

—William Shenstone

I have never been nervous in all my life and I have no patience with people who are. If you know what you are going to do, you have no reason to be nervous. And I knew what I was going to do.

—Mary Garden

All men are afraid in battle. The coward is the one who lets his fear overcome his sense of duty. Duty is the essence of manhood.

—General George S. Patton

Be Confident (But Not Arrogant)

First thing every morning before you arise
say out loud, "I believe," three times.
—Ovid

Women who are confident of their abilities
are more likely to succeed than those who
lack confidence, even though the latter may
be much more competent and talented and
industrious.
—Dr. Joyce Brothers

Make yourself indispensable and you'll be
moved up. Act as if you're indispensable
and you'll be moved out.
—Jules Ormont

To be a champ, you have to believe in
yourself when nobody else will.
—Sugar Ray Robinson

If you think you can, you can. And if you
think you can't, you're right.
—Mary Kay Ash

The barrier between success is not something which exists in the real world: it is composed purely and simply of doubts about ability.

—Franklin D. Roosevelt

Life is not easy for any of us. But what of that? We must have perseverance and above all confidence in ourselves. We must believe that we are gifted for something, and that this thing, at whatever cost, must be attained.

—Marie Curie

Believe in yourself! Have faith in your abilities! Without a humble but reasonable confidence in your own powers you cannot be successful or happy.

—Norman Vincent Peale

As is our confidence, so is our capacity.

—William Hazlitt

Have confidence that if you have done a little thing well, you can do a bigger thing well too.

—David Storey

YOU ARE WHAT YOU BELIEVE

And above all things, never think that you're
not good enough yourself. A man should
never think that. My belief is that in life
people will take you at your own reckoning.
—Anthony Trollope

Every person is the creation of himself, the
image of his own thinking and believing. As
individuals think and believe, so they are.
—Claude M. Bristol

The lack of belief is a defect that ought to
be concealed when it cannot be overcome.
—Jonathan Swift

I am not a has-been. I'm a will-be.
—Lauren Bacall

The will to do springs from the knowledge
that we can do.
—James Allen

SET GOALS FOR YOURSELF AND YOU'LL ACHIEVE THEM

Skill and confidence are an unconquered army.
—George Herbert

You can change your beliefs so they empower your dreams and desires.
—Marcia Wieder

I probably hold the distinction of being one movie star who, by all laws of logic, should never have made it. At each stage of my career, I lacked the experience.
—Audrey Hepburn

Nothing is too difficult—you only need to know how.
—Yiddish proverb

If we want a free and peaceful world, if we want to make the deserts bloom and man grow to greater dignity as a human being— we can do it.
—Eleanor Roosevelt

FOLLOW YOUR HEART

Some believe all that parents, tutors, and kindred believe. They take their principles by inheritance, and defend them as they would their estates, because they are born heirs to them.

—Alan W. Watts

When the intensity of emotional conviction subsides, a man who is in the habit of reasoning will search for logical grounds in favor of the belief which he finds in himself.

—Bertrand Russell

Life involves passions, faiths, doubts, and courage.

—Josiah Royce

Some of the finest moral intuitions come to quite humble people. The visiting of lofty ideas doesn't depend on formal schooling.

—Alfred North Whitehead

Yes, I have doubted. I have wandered off the path, but I always return. It is intuitive, an intrinsic, built-in sense of direction. I seem always to find my way home.

—Helen Hayes

Every time a resolve or fine glow of feeling evaporates without bearing fruit, it is worse than a chance lost; it works to hinder future emotions from taking the normal path of discharge.

—William James

The world may take your reputation from you, but it cannot take your character.

—Emma Dunham Kelley

One person with a belief is equal to a force of ninety-nine who have only interests.

—John Stuart Mill

A goose flies by a chart the Royal Geographical Society could not improve.

—Oliver Wendell Holmes

BE PROUD, BUT OUTWARDLY HUMBLE

Who I am is the best I can be.
> —Leontyne Price

It is always the secure who are humble.
> —Gilbert Keith Chesterton

Oh, I'm so inadequate. And I love myself!
> —Meg Ryan

Believing in our hearts that who we are is enough is the key to a more satisfying and balanced life.
> —Ellen Sue Stern

Living with a saint is more grueling than being one.
> —Robert Neville

Success has nothing to do with what you gain in life or accomplish for yourself. It's what you do for others.
> —Danny Thomas

EXERCISING
SELF-RESTRAINT

DON'T MEDDLE

Everybody's business is nobody's business,
and nobody's business is my business.
—Clara Barton

What it lies in our power to do, it lies in
our power not to do.
—Aristotle

I listen and give input only if somebody asks.
—Barbara Bush

A good example is the best sermon.
—Anon.

Often we can help each other most by
leaving each other alone.
—Elbert Hubbard

If two friends ask you to judge a dispute,
don't accept, because you will lose one
friend.
—St. Augustine

Don't Take Yourself Too Seriously

There is a difference between conceit and confidence. Conceit is bragging about yourself. Confidence means you believe you can get the job done.

—Johnny Unitas

It is far more impressive when others discover your good qualities without your help.

—Judith Martin (Miss Manners)

In our society those who are in reality superior in intelligence can be accepted by their fellows only if they pretend they are not.

—Marya Mannes

Wise men don't need advice. Fools don't take it.

—Benjamin Franklin

A fellow who is always declaring he's no fool usually has his suspicions.

—Wilson Mizner

The man who is ostentatious of his modesty is twin to the statue that wears a fig-leaf.
—Mark Twain

Knowledge alone is not enough. It must be leavened with magnanimity before it becomes wisdom.
—Adlai E. Stevenson

More people are ruined by victory, I imagine, than by defeat.
—Eleanor Roosevelt

The more important the title, the more self-important the person, the greater the amount of time spent on the Eastern shuttle, the more suspicious the man and the less vitality in the organization.
—Jane O'Reilly

A man doesn't begin to attain wisdom until he recognizes that he is no longer indispensable.
—Admiral Richard Byrd

Half of the harm that is done in this world is due to people who want to feel important. They don't mean to do harm. But the harm does not interest them.

—T. S. Eliot

Vanity is the quicksand of reason.

—George Sand

My importance to the world is relatively small. On the other hand, my importance to myself is tremendous. I am all I have to work with, to play with, to suffer and to enjoy. It is not the eyes of others that I am wary of, but of my own. I do not intend to let myself down more than I can possibly help, and I find that the fewer illusions I have about myself or the world around me, the better company I am for myself.

—Noel Coward

Nonsense is so good only because common sense is so limited.

—George Santayana

DON'T OVERDO IT

Be content with your lot; one cannot be first in everything.

—Aesop

Gammy used to say, "Too much scrubbing takes the life right out of things."

—Betty MacDonald

To wear your heart on your sleeve isn't a very good plan; you should wear it inside, where it functions best.

—Margaret Thatcher

Do not spoil what you have by desiring what you have not; but remember that what you now have was once among the things you only hoped for.

—Epicurus

I know too well the poison and the sting of things too sweet.

—Adelaide Proctor

Who is apt, on occasion, to assign a
multitude of reasons when one will do?
This is a sure sign of weakness in argument.
—Harriet Martineau

Ask the gods nothing excessive.
—Aeschylus
The point of good writing is knowing when
to stop.
—L. M. Montgomery

We always weaken whatever we exaggerate.
—Jean François de La Harpe

A wise man will live as much within his wit
as his income.
—Philip Dormer Stanhope,
Earl of Chesterfield

Transformation also means looking for ways
to stop pushing yourself so hard
professionally or inviting so much stress.
—Gail Sheehy

A position of eminence makes a great
person greater and a small person less.
                                    —Jean De La Bruyère

Superior people never make long visits.
                                    —Marianne Moore

A short saying oft contains much wisdom.
                                    —Sophocles

The longest absence is less perilous to love
than the terrible trials of incessant proximity.
                                    —Ouida

Never eat more than you can lift.
                                    —Miss Piggy

We never repent of having eaten too little.
                                    —Thomas Jefferson

Hope for a miracle. But don't depend on
one.
                                    —Talmud

DON'T WORRY ABOUT THINGS YOU CAN'T CONTROL

A wise man cares not for what he cannot have.

—Anon.

You always feel when you look it straight in the eye that you could have put more into it, could have let yourself go and dug harder.

—Emily Carr

There's only one corner of the universe you can be certain of improving, and that's your own self.

—Aldous Huxley

To create is to boggle the mind and alter the mood. Once the urge has surged, it maintains its own momentum. We may go along for the ride, but when we attempt to steer the course, the momentum dies.

—Sue Atchley Ebaugh

DON'T PASS JUDGMENT

A critic is someone who never actually goes to the battle, yet who afterwards comes out shooting the wounded.

—Tyne Daly

He that has no fools, knaves, nor beggars in his family was begot by a flash of lightning.

—Thomas Fuller

Sainthood is acceptable only in saints.

—Pamela Hansford Johnson

He that will have a perfect brother must resign himself to remaining brotherless.

—Italian proverb

When nobody around you seems to measure up, it's time to check your yardstick.

—Bill Lemley

DON'T HOLD GRUDGES

Grace fills empty spaces, but it can only
enter where there is a void to receive it, and
it is grace itself which makes this void.
                                        —Simone Weil

Forgiveness is the act of admitting we are
like other people.
                                        —Christina Baldwin

To err is human, to forgive divine.
                                        —Alexander Pope

The weak can never forgive. Forgiveness is
the attribute of the strong.
                                        —Italian proverb

A man must learn to forgive himself.
                                        —Arthur Davis Ficke

We are cold to others only when we are dull
in ourselves.
                                        —William Hazlitt

HAVE REALISTIC EXPECTATIONS

People seek within a short span of life to satisfy a thousand desires, each of which is insatiable.

—Oliver Goldsmith

One cannot collect all the beautiful shells on the beach.

—Anne Morrow Lindbergh

What is destructive is impatience, haste, expecting too much too fast.

—May Sarton

If it goes, it goes. Don't force it.

—Yiddish proverb

The attainment of an ideal is often the beginning of a disillusion.

—Stanley Baldwin

Don't try to teach a whole course in one lesson.

—Kathryn Murray

No folly is more costly than the folly of intolerant idealism.

—Winston Churchill

Idealism increases in direct proportion to one's distance from the problem.

—John Galsworthy

The whole point of getting things done is knowing what to leave undone.

—Lady Stella Reading

If we could learn how to balance rest against effort, calmness against strain, quiet against turmoil, we would assure ourselves of joy in living and psychological health for life.

—Josephine Rathbone

An idealist is one who, on noticing that a rose smells better than a cabbage, concludes that it is also more nourishing.

—H. L. Mencken

BE PATIENT

The bird of paradise alights only upon the hand that does not grasp.

—John Berry

To lose patience is to lose the battle.

—Mahatma Gandhi

The most potent and sacred command which can be laid upon any artist is the command: wait.

—Iris Murdoch

A man must learn to endure patiently what he cannot avoid conveniently.

—Michel de Montaigne

Patience is the companion of wisdom.

—St. Augustine

Panic is not an effective long-term organizing strategy.

—Starhawk

BE CONSIDERATE OF OTHERS

Whoever gossips to you will gossip of you.
—Spanish proverb

If we would build on a sure foundation in friendship, we must love friends for their sake rather than for our own.
—Charlotte Brontë

There is a world of practical religion in simply being considerate of others.
—Roger Babson

Tact is the knack of making a point without making an enemy.
—Sir Isaac Newton

Tact is the art of convincing people that they know more than you do.
—Raymond Mortimer

SILENCE IS GOLDEN

He has occasional flashes of silence that
make his conversation perfectly delightful.
                                    —Sydney Smith

The silence of a man who loves to praise is
a censure sufficiently severe.
                                    —Charlotte Lennox

A word out of season may mar a whole
lifetime.
                                    —Greek proverb

Silence is one of the great arts of conversation.
                                    —Hannah More

When you have nothing to say, say nothing.
                                    —Charles Caleb Colton

BE CAREFUL WHAT YOU SAY

He who praises everybody praises nobody.
—Dr. Samuel Johnson

A gossip is one who talks to you about
others; a bore is one who talks to you about
himself; and a brilliant conversationalist is
one who talks to you about yourself.
—Lisa Kirk

Education commences at the mother's knee,
and every word spoken within hearsay of
little children tends toward the formation of
character.
—Hosea Ballou

A statement once let loose cannot be caught
by four horses.
—Japanese proverb

Minimum information given with
maximum politeness.
—Jacqueline Kennedy Onassis

TAKING CONTROL
OF YOUR LIFE

Expect More from Life

The quality of a person's life is in direct proportion to his commitment to excellence, regardless of his chosen field of endeavor.
—Vince Lombardi

It is not opposition but indifference which separates men.
—Mary Parker Follett

If you expect nothing, you're apt to be surprised. You'll get it.
—Malcolm S. Forbes

I have always had a dread of becoming a passenger in life.
—Margareth II, Queen of Denmark

High expectations are the key to everything.
—Sam Walton

A continued atmosphere of hectic passion is very trying if you haven't got any of your own.
—Dorothy L. Sayers

Vision + Enthusiasm = Success

The condition of the most passionate
enthusiast is to be preferred over the
individual who, because of the fear of
making a mistake, won't in the end affirm
or deny anything.
                                    —Thomas Carlyle

If you really want something you can figure
out how to make it happen.
                                    —Cher

Flaming enthusiasm, backed up by horse
sense and persistence, is the quality that
most frequently makes for success.
                                    —Dale Carnegie

Never be afraid to sit awhile and think.
                                    —Lorraine Hansbury

Enthusiasm is the inspiration of everything
great. Without it no man is to be feared,
and with it none despised.
                                    —Christian Nevell Bovee

Nothing is so contagious as enthusiasm.
                    —Samuel Taylor Coleridge

I will not be just a tourist in the world of
images, just watching images passing by
which I cannot live in, make love to, possess
as permanent sources of joy and ecstasy.
                    —Anaïs Nin

Enthusiasm is a vital element toward the
individual success of every man or woman.
                    —Conrad Hilton

Enthusiasm moves the world.
                    —Arthur James Balfour

You can't sweep other people off their feet if
you can't be swept off your own.
                    —Clarence Day

Enthusiasm is the genius of sincerity and
truth accomplishes no victories without it.
                    —Edward G. Bulwer-Lytton

DON'T LEAVE YOUR FUTURE IN THE HANDS OF OTHERS

I don't follow precedent, I establish it.
—Fanny Ellen Holtzman

There is no such thing as vicarious experience.
—Mary Parker Follett

You need to overcome the tug of people against you as you reach for high goals.
—General George S. Patton

I never really address myself to any image anybody has of me. That's like fighting with ghosts.
—Sally Field

Every man must get to heaven his own way.
—Frederick the Great

You have to deal with the fact that your life is your life.
—Alex Hailey

DON'T BE FATALISTIC

I got well by talking. Death could not get a word in edgewise, grew discouraged, and traveled on.

—Louise Erdrich

I was forced to live far beyond my years when just a child, now I have reversed the order and I intend to remain young indefinitely.

—Mary Pickford

You are in the driver's seat of your life and can point your life down any road you want to travel. You can go as fast or as slow as you want to go ... and you can change the road you're on at any time.

—Jinger Heath

The history of free men is never really written by chance but by choice; their choice!

—Dwight D. Eisenhower

LIFE IS WHAT YOU MAKE IT

In the arena of life the honors and rewards
fall to those who show their good qualities
in action.
> —Aristotle

There is no scientific answer for success.
You can't define it. You've simply got to live
it and do it.
> —Anita Roddick

The winds and waves are always on the side
of the ablest navigators.
> —Edward Gibbon

Boredom is a sickness of the soul.
> —Anon.

You need to claim the events in your life to
make yourself yours. When you truly possess
all you have been and done, which may take
some time, you are fierce with reality.
> —Florida Scott-Maxwell

BE YOURSELF

There is only one success—to be able to
spend your life in your own way.
—Christopher Morley

Borrowed thoughts, like borrowed money,
only show the poverty of the borrower.
—Lady Marguerite Blessington

An endeavor to please elders is at the
bottom of high marks and mediocre careers.
—John Jay Chapman

Those people who are uncomfortable in
themselves are disagreeable to others.
—William Hazlitt

You were once wild here. Don't let them
tame you!
—Isadora Duncan

No person has the right to rain on your
dreams.
—Marian Wright Edelman

There is overwhelming evidence that the higher the level of self-esteem, the more likely one will treat others with respect, kindness, and generosity.

—Nathaniel Branden

Accept the place the divine providence has found for you.

—Ralph Waldo Emerson

If you make friends with yourself you will never be alone.

—Maxwell Maltz

Too many people overvalue what they are not and undervalue what they are.

—Malcolm Forbes

Learn what you are and be such.

—Pindar

If God had wanted me otherwise, he would have created me otherwise.

—Johann von Goethe

KNOWING WHAT
REALLY MATTERS

THE LITTLE PLEASURES OF LIFE

There is nothing like staying at home for real comfort.

—Jane Austen

Moderation. Small helpings. Sample a little bit of everything. These are the secrets of happiness and good health.

—Julia Child

There are half hours that dilate to the importance of centuries.

—Mary Catherwood

A thing of beauty is a joy forever.

—John Keats

Anyone who's a great kisser I'm always interested in.

—Cher

Teach us delight in simple things.

—Rudyard Kipling

What would life be without art? Science prolongs life. To consist of what—eating, drinking, and sleeping? What is the good of living longer if it is only a matter of satisfying the requirements that sustain life? All this is nothing without the charm of art.
—Sarah Bernhardt

Whatever I am offered in devotion with a pure heart—a leaf, a flower, fruit, or water—I accept with joy.
—Bhagavad Gita

Our life is frittered away by detail…. Simplify, simplify.
—Henry David Thoreau

The art of art, the glory of expression, and the sunshine of the light of letters, is simplicity.
—Walt Whitman

NOT POSSESSIONS, BUT A LIFE WELL LIVED

Riches are not from abundance of worldly
goods, but from a contented mind.
                                    —Muhammad

Prosperity is only an instrument to be used,
not a deity to be worshiped.
                                    —Calvin Coolidge

Truth is like heat or light; its vibrations are
endless, and are endlessly felt.
                                    —Margaret Deland

A cynic is a man who knows the price of
everything and the value of nothing.
                                    —Oscar Wilde

It is not the man who has too little, but the
man who craves more, that is poor.
                                    —Seneca

What we need most, is not so much to
realize the ideal as to idealize the real.
                                    —Francis Herbert Hedge

True contentment depends not upon what we have; a tub was large enough for Diogenes, but a world was too little for Alexander.

—Charles Caleb Colton

No one has yet had the courage to memorialize his wealth on his tombstone. A dollar mark would not look well there.

—Corra May Harris

Those who intend on becoming great should love neither themselves or their own things, but only what is just, whether it happens to be done by themselves or others.

—Plato

My mother drew a distinction between achievement and success. She said that achievement is the knowledge that you have studied and worked hard and done the best that is in you. Success is being praised by others. That is nice but not as important or satisfying. Always aim for achievement and forget about success.

—Helen Hayes

FRIENDS, FAMILY, AND THE RESPECT OF OTHERS

Men are what their mothers made them.
                    —Ralph Waldo Emerson

The darn trouble with cleaning the house is it gets dirty the next day anyway, so skip a week if you have to. The children are the most important thing.
                    —Barbara Bush

It's the friends you can call up at 4:00 a.m. that matter.
                    —Marlene Dietrich

I figure if I have my health, can pay the rent and I have my friends, I call it "content."
                    —Lauren Bacall

The best rule of friendship is to keep your heart a little softer than your head.
                    —Anon.

If a man does not make new acquaintances as he advances through life, he will soon find himself left alone. A man should keep his friendships in constant repair.

—Samuel Johnson

You leave home to seek your fortune and, when you get it, you go home and share it with your family.

—Anita Baker

Better a hundred enemies outside the house than one inside.

—Arabic proverb

The ornament of a house is the friends who frequent it.

—Ralph Waldo Emerson

The family is the nucleus of civilization.

—William Durant

BEING TRUE TO
ONE'S VISION AND PRINCIPLES

Man's main task in life is to give birth to himself.

—Erich Fromm

A puff of wind and popular praise weigh the same.

—English proverb

The most comprehensive formulation of therapeutic goals is the striving for wholeheartedness: to be without pretense, to be emotionally sincere, to be able to put the whole of oneself into one's feelings, one's work, one's beliefs.

—Karen Horney

We are traditionally rather proud of ourselves for having slipped creative work in there between the domestic chores and obligations. I'm not sure we deserve such big A-pluses for all that.

—Toni Morrison

When you cease to dream you cease to live.
—Malcolm S. Forbes

Many persons have a wrong idea of what constitutes real happiness. It is not obtained through self-gratification but through fidelity to a worthy purpose.
—Helen Keller

I felt as if I were walking with destiny, and that all my past life had been but a preparation for this hour and this trial.
—Winston Churchill

Man has no nobler function than to defend the truth.
—Mahalia Jackson

It's faith in something and enthusiasm for something that makes life worth living.
—Oliver Wendell Holmes

We may be personally defeated, but our principles, never.
—William Lloyd Garrison

DOING THE BEST WE CAN

Ambition is destruction, only competence matters.

—Jill Robinson

Someone once asked me what I regarded as the three most important requirements for happiness. My answer was: "A feeling that you have been honest with yourself and those around you; a feeling that you have done the best you could both in your personal life and in your work; and the ability to love others."

—Eleanor Roosevelt

If a man has done his best, what else is there?

—General George S. Patton

The power I exert on the court depends on the power of my arguments, not on my gender.

—Sandra Day O'Connor

The struggle alone pleases us, not the victory.

—Blaise Pascal

Love and Compassion

Whatever you do, stamp out abuses, and
love those who love you.
—Voltaire

Love and respect are the most important
aspects of parenting, and of all relationships.
—Jodie Foster

The supreme happiness of life is the
conviction that we are loved.
—Victor Hugo

Just pray for a tough hide and a tender heart.
—Ruth Graham

When a good man is hurt all who would be
called good must suffer with him.
—Euripides

Yet, taught by time, my heart has learned to
glow for other's good, and melt at other's woe.
—Homer

IT'S WHAT INSIDE THAT COUNTS

Greatness and goodness are not means, but
ends.
>—Samuel Taylor Coleridge

The fatal metaphor of progress, which
means leaving things behind us, has utterly
obscured the real idea of growth, which
means leaving things inside us.
>—Gilbert Keith Chesterton

Goodness is the only investment that never
fails.
>—Henry David Thoreau

There is only one history of any
importance, and it is the history of what
you once believed in, and the history of
what you came to believe in.
>—Kay Boyle

It doesn't help your five-iron if you're pretty.
>—Laura Baugh

I've never sought success in order to get fame and money; it's the talent and the passion that count in success.
—Ingrid Bergman

Love built on beauty, soon as beauty, dies.
—John Donne

Neither smiles nor frowns, neither good intentions nor harsh words, are a substitute for strength.
—John F. Kennedy

We all lose our looks eventually, better develop your character and interest in life.
—Jacqueline Bisset

No amount of ability is of the slightest avail without honor.
—Andrew Carnegie

I am happy and content because I think I am.
—Alain-René Lesage

EXPERIENCE AND ACHIEVEMENT

Nothing ever becomes real till it is
experienced—even a proverb is no proverb
to you till your life has illustrated it.
                              —John Keats

Where I was born and where and how I
have lived is unimportant. It is what I have
done with where I have been that should be
of interest.
                              —Georgia O'Keefe

Experience is what really happens to you in
the long run; the truth that finally overtakes
you.
                              —Katherine Anne Porter

We judge ourselves by what we feel capable
of doing, while others judge us by what we
have already done.
                              —Henry Wadsworth Longfellow

WORK, CAREER, AND
LOVING WHAT YOU DO

It is the greatest shot of adrenaline to be
doing what you've wanted to do so badly.
—Charles Lindbergh

Neither woman nor man lives by work, or
love, alone....The human self defines itself
and grows through love and work: All
psychology before and after Freud boils
down to that.
—Betty Friedan

Blessed is he who has found his life's work;
let him ask no other blessedness.
—Thomas Carlyle

Work is creativity accompanied by the
comforting realization that one is bringing
forth something really good and necessary,
with a conviction that a sudden, arbitrary
cessation would cause a sensitive void,
produce a loss.
—Jenny Heynrichs

Happiness is mostly a byproduct of doing what makes us feel fulfilled.
—Benjamin Spock

The medals don't mean anything and the glory doesn't last. It's all about your happiness. The rewards are going to come, but my happiness is just loving the sport and having fun performing.
—Jackie Joyner-Kersee

Type faster.
—Isaac Asimov, when asked what he would do if he only had six months to live

The simple idea that everyone needs a reasonable amount of challenging work in his or her life, and also a personal life, complete with noncompetitive leisure, has never really taken hold.
—Judith Martin (Miss Manners)

The happy people are those who are producing something.
—William Ralph Inge

It is only when I am doing my work that I am truly alive.

—Federico Fellini

He who labors diligently need never despair, for all things are accomplished by diligence and labor.

—Menander

Never desert your own line of talent. Be what nature intended you for, and you will succeed.

—Sydney Smith

They are happy men whose natures sort with their vocations.

—Francis Bacon

Work and play are words used to describe the same thing under differing conditions.

—Mark Twain

ACCEPTING RESPONSIBILITY

It's Up to You to Make Things Happen

Deliberation is the work of many men.
Action, of one alone.
> —Charles de Gaulle

The spirit of self-help is the root of all
genuine growth in the individual.
> —Samuel Smiles

Any committee is only as good as the most
knowledgeable, determined, and vigorous
person on it. There must be somebody who
provides the flame.
> —Lady Bird Johnson

My father instilled in me that if you don't see
things happening the way you want them to,
you get out there and make them happen.
> —Susan Powter

No bird soars too high if he soars with his
own wings.
> —William Blake

DON'T POINT FINGERS

Believe there is a great power silently
working all things for good, behave yourself
and never mind the rest.

—Beatrix Potter

There's man all over for you, blaming on
his boots the fault of his feet.

—Samuel Beckett

I made the decision. I'm accountable.

—Janet Reno

A man can get discouraged many times but
he is not a failure until he begins to blame
somebody else and stops trying.

—John Burroughs

We have not passed the subtle line between
childhood and adulthood until ... we have
stopped saying "It got lost," and say, "I lost
it."

—Sydney J. Harris

REMEMBER THAT OTHERS
RELY ON AND LOOK UP TO YOU

Let everyone who has the grace of
intelligence fear that, because of it, he will
be judged more heavily if he is negligent.
—St. Bridget of Sweden

The essence of greatness is neglect of the self.
—James Anthony Froude

Service to others is the rent you pay for
living on this planet.
—Marian Wright Edelman

You don't live in a world all your own. Your
brothers are here, too.
—Albert Schweitzer

A helping word to one in trouble is often
like a switch in a railroad track ... an inch
between a wreck and smooth, rolling
prosperity.
—Henry Ward Beecher

DON'T COMPLAIN OR CRITICIZE

If you have no will to change it, you have no will to criticize it.

—Anon.

It's better to light a candle than curse the darkness.

—Eleanor Roosevelt

Both tears and sweat are salty, but they render a different result. Tears will get you sympathy; sweat will get you change.

—Jesse Jackson

It was completely fruitless to quarrel with the world, whereas the quarrel with oneself was occasionally fruitful and always, she had to admit, interesting.

—May Sarton

The pessimist is half-licked before he starts.

—Thomas A. Buckner

DON'T JUST TALK—ACT

A person of words and not of deeds is like a
garden full of weeds.

—Anon.

What we learn we learn by doing.

—Aristotle

It's where we go, and what we do when we
get there, that tells us who we are.

—Joyce Carol Oates

He who desires, but acts not, breeds
pestilence.

—William Blake

There can be no happiness if the things we
believe in are different from the things we do.

—Freya Stark

It's dogged as does it. It ain't thinking about it.

—Anthony Trollope

If women want any rights more than they got, why don't they just take them and not be talking about it?

—Sojourner Truth

Words without actions are the assassins of idealism.

—Herbert Hoover

I would not sit waiting for some value tomorrow, nor for something to happen. One could wait a lifetime.... I would *make* something happen.

—Louis L'Amour

The amount of satisfaction you get from life depends largely on your own ingenuity, self-sufficiency, and resourcefulness. People who wait around for life to supply their satisfaction usually find boredom instead.

—Dr. William Menninger

A meowing cat catches no mice.

—Yiddish proverb

HELP COMES TO THOSE WHO HELP THEMSELVES

To have a curable illness and to leave it untreated except for prayer is like sticking your hand in a fire and asking God to remove the flame.

—Sandra L. Douglas

Chop your own wood, and it will warm you twice.

—Henry Ford

It is not our circumstances that create our discontent or contentment. It is us.

—Vivian Greene

The first requisite of a good citizen in this republic of ours is that he shall be able and willing to pull his weight.

—Theodore Roosevelt

Mankind's greatest gift is that we have free choice.

—Elisabeth Kübler-Ross

DON'T SHRINK
FROM A CHALLENGE

You have to do what you love to do, not get stuck in that comfort zone of a regular job. Life is not a dress rehearsal. This is it.
—Lucinda Basset

If the sky falls, hold up your hands.
—Spanish proverb

I used to believe that marriage would diminish me, reduce my options. That you had to be someone less to live with someone else when, of course, you have to be someone more.
—Candice Bergen

You can do anything in this world if you are prepared to take the consequences.
—W. Somerset Maugham

DOING THE RIGHT THING

BEING TRUTHFUL

Show me a liar, and I'll show you a thief.
—George Herbert

The elegance of honesty needs no adornment.
—Merry Browne

An honest man's word is as good as his bond.
—Cervantes

Nothing astonishes men so much as common sense and plain dealing.
—Ralph Waldo Emerson

Truth is always exciting. Speak it, then; life is dull without it.
—Pearl S. Buck

And ye shall know the truth, and the truth shall make you free.
—John 8:32

You cannot weave truth on a loom of lies.
—Suzette Haden Elgin

Honesty is the first chapter in the book of wisdom.
                                    —Thomas Jefferson

A "no" uttered from deepest conviction is better and greater than a "yes" merely uttered to please, or what is worse, to avoid trouble.
                                    —Mahatma Gandhi

A lie travels round the world while truth is putting her boots on.
                                    —French proverb

Candor is a proof of both a just frame of mind, and of a good tone of breeding. It is a quality that belongs equally to the honest man and to the gentleman.
                                    —James F. Cooper

Friends, if we be honest with ourselves, we shall be honest with each other.
                                    —George Macdonald

Earnestness and sincerity are synonymous.
                                    —Corita Kent

STICKING TO YOUR PRINCIPLES

When people base their lives on principle, 99 percent of their decisions are already made.
—Anon.

We shall return to proven ways—not because they are old, but because they are true.
—Barry Goldwater

What's got badly, goes badly.
—Irish proverb

Always be ready to speak your mind, and a base man will avoid you.
—William Blake

Conscience, as I understand it, is the impulse to do the right thing because it is right, regardless of personal ends, and has nothing whatever to do with the ability to distinguish between right and wrong.
—Margaret Collier Graham

LOOKING OUT FOR OTHERS

Recompense injury with justice, and
recompense kindness with kindness.
                    —Confucius

As long as you keep a person down, some
part of you has to be down there to hold
him down, so it means you cannot soar as
you otherwise might.
                    —Marian Anderson

Human kindness has never weakened the
stamina or softened the fiber of a free
people. A nation does not have to be cruel
to be tough.
                    —Franklin D. Roosevelt

I hear much of people's calling out to
punish the guilty, but very few are
concerned to clear the innocent.
                    —Daniel Defoe

REALIZING THE
CONSEQUENCES OF YOUR ACTIONS

Authority without wisdom is like a heavy axe without an edge, fitter to bruise than to polish.

—Anne Bradstreet

Add not fire to fire.

—Greek proverb

Life is for one generation. A good name is forever.

—Japanese proverb

Our deeds still travel with us from afar, and what we have been makes us what we are.

—George Eliot

It is easy—terribly easy—to shake a man's faith in himself. To take advantage of that, to break a man's spirit, is devil's work.

—George Bernard Shaw

MAKING GOOD CHOICES

Fear is the parent of cruelty.
                    —James Anthony Froude

There is always a time to make right what is
wrong.
                    —Susan Griffin

The time is always right to do what is right.
                    —Martin Luther King, Jr.

Lawlessness is a self-perpetuating, ever-
expanding habit.
                    —Dorothy Thompson

Excellence is an art won by training and
habituation. We do not act rightly because
we have virtue or excellence, but we rather
have those because we have acted rightly.
We are what we repeatedly do.
                    —Aristotle

All sins are attempts to fill voids.
                    —Simone Weil

BEING TRUE TO YOURSELF

So long as men praise you, you can only be sure that you are not yet on your own true path but on someone else's.
—Friedrich Wilhem Nietzsche

A guilty conscience is a hidden enemy.
—American Indian proverb

The first and worst of all frauds is to cheat one's self. All sin is easy after that.
—Pearl Bailey

Rules of society are nothing; one's conscience is the umpire.
—Madame Dudevant

It is better to deserve honors and not have them than to have them and not deserve them.
—Mark Twain

LEARNING TO SHARE AND GIVE

Generosity lies less in giving much than in giving at the right moment.
—Jean De La Bruyère

Generosity is the flower of justice.
—Nathaniel Hawthorne

No person was ever honored for what he received. Honor has been the reward for what he gave.
—Calvin Coolidge

Measure thy life by loss instead of gain, Not by the wine drunk, but by the wine poured forth.
—Harriet King

Purposeful giving is not as apt to deplete one's resources; it belongs to that natural order of giving that seems to renew itself even in the act of depletion.
—Anne Morrow Lindbergh

He who gives what he would as readily throw away, gives without generosity; for the essence of generosity is in self sacrifice.

—Sir Henry Taylor

Generosity with strings is not generosity: it is a deal.

—Marya Mannes

You give but little when you give of your possessions. It is when you give of yourself that you truly give.

—Kahlil Gibran

He who gives while he lives gets to know where it goes.

—Percy Ross

It is another's fault if he be ungrateful, but it is mine if I do not give. To find one thankful man, I will oblige a great many that are not so.

—Seneca

FORGIVING OTHERS

Forgiveness is not an occasional act: it is an attitude.
> —Martin Luther King, Jr.

Forgiveness is the act of admitting we are like other people.
> —Christina Baldwin

Forgiveness is an act of the will, and the will can function regardless of the temperature of the heart.
> —Corrie Ten Boom

The weak can never forgive. Forgiveness is the attribute of the strong.
> —Mahatma Gandhi

The stupid neither forgive nor forget; the naive forgive and forget; the wise forgive, but do not forget.
> —Thomas Szasz

LIVING YOUR IDEALS

Remember, no effort that we make to attain
something beautiful is ever lost.
—Helen Keller

What distinguishes the majority of men
from the few is their inability to act
according to their beliefs.
—John Stuart Mill

Faced with crisis, the man of character falls
back on himself. He imposes his own stamp
of action, takes responsibility for it, makes
it his own.
—Charles De Gaulle

It's not dying for faith that's so hard, it's
living up to it.
—William M. Thackeray

Our ideals are our better selves.
—Amos Bronson Alcott

BEING THANKFUL

A thankful heart is the parent of all virtues.
—Cicero

No duty is more urgent than that of
returning thanks.
—St. Ambrose

Thankfulness is the beginning of gratitude.
Gratitude is the completion of thankfulness.
Thankfulness may consist merely of words.
Gratitude is shown in acts.
—Henri Frederic Amiel

Gratitude is a twofold love—love coming to
visit us, and love running out to greet a
welcome guest.
—Henry Van Dyke

Gratitude is a duty which ought to be paid,
but which none have a right to expect.
—Jean Jacques Rousseau

ADMIT WHEN
YOU'RE WRONG

Quarrels would not last so long if the fault were only on one side.
> —François de La Rochefoucauld

Nothing has an uglier look to us than reason, when it is not on our side.
> —George Savile, Marquess de Halifax

Ah, how steadily do they who are guilty shrink from reproof!
> —Amelia Jenks Bloomer

I've arrived at this outermost edge of my life by my own actions. Where I am is thoroughly unacceptable. Therefore, I must stop doing what I have been doing.
> —Alice Koller

To make no mistake is not in the power of man; but from their errors and mistakes the wise and good learn wisdom for the future.
> —Plutarch

WITH GOOD FORTUNE
COMES RESPONSIBILITY

For unto whomsoever much is given, of him shall be much required.

—Luke 12:48

To be born free is an accident; to live free a responsibility; to die free is an obligation.

—Mrs. Hubbard Davis

The price of greatness is responsibility.

—Winston Churchill

God gives the nuts, but He does not crack them.

—German proverb

CHANGING THE WAY YOU LOOK AT THINGS

LET GO OF THE PAST

Do not look back in anger, or forward in fear, but around in awareness.

—James Thurber

Those who can't forget are worse off than those who can't remember.

—Anon.

Just do your best today and tomorrow will come—tomorrow's going to be a busy day, a happy day.

—Helen Boehm

The man who views the world at fifty the same as he did at twenty has wasted thirty years of his life.

—Muhammad Ali

"The good old days." The only good days are ahead.

—Alice Childress

SHRUG IT OFF

Keep your sense of humor. There's enough
stress in the rest of your life to let bad shots
ruin a game you're supposed to enjoy.
—Amy Alcott

Things turn out best for people who make
the best of the way things turn out.
—Anon.

Learn to laugh at your troubles and you'll
never run out of things to laugh at.
—Lyn Karol

For a just man falleth seven times, and
riseth up again.
—Proverbs 24:16

If I lose, I'll walk away and never feel bad....
Because I did all I could do, there was
nothing more to do.
—Joe Frazier

STAY OPTIMISTIC

The crisis of today is the joke of tomorrow.
—H. G. Wells

Humor is the healthy way of feeling "distance" between one's self and the problem, a way of standing off and looking at one's problems with perspective.
—Rollo May

Optimism doesn't wait on facts. It deals with prospects.
—Norman Cousins

I've always believed that you can think positive just as well as you can think negative.
—James A. Baldwin

It is worth a thousand pounds a year to have the habit of looking on the bright side of things.
—Samuel Johnson

FAILURE IS
NOT AN OPTION

Nothing can stop the man with the right
mental attitude from achieving his goal;
nothing on earth can help the man with the
wrong mental attitude.

—Thomas Jefferson

Some of my best friends are illusions. Been
sustaining me for years.

—Sheila Ballantyne

Be a "how" thinker, not an "if" thinker.

—Anon.

Without faith, nothing is possible. With it,
nothing is impossible.

—Mary McLeod Bethune

As long as a person doesn't admit he's
defeated, he is not defeated—he's just a
little behind, and isn't through fighting.

—Darrell Royal

FOCUS ON THE GOOD THINGS

Some people are always grumbling because roses have thorns; I am thankful that thorns have roses.

—Alphonse Karr

But here's what I've learned in this war, in this country, in this city: to love the miracle of having been born.

—Oriana Fallaci

The really happy person is the one who can enjoy the scenery on a detour.

—Anon.

Sometimes I found that in my happy moments I could not believe that I had ever been miserable.

—Joanna Field

Goodness is easier to recognize than to define.

—W. H. Auden

SET YOUR GOALS HIGHER

If you would hit the mark, you must aim a little above it.
> —Henry Wadsworth Longfellow

We have believed—and we do believe now—that freedom is indivisible, that peace is indivisible, that economic prosperity is indivisible.
> —Indira Gandhi

There is always room at the top.
> —Daniel Webster

I always ask the question, "Is this what I want in my life?"
> —Kathy Ireland

In the long run men hit only what they aim at. Therefore, though they should fall immediately, they had better aim at something high.
> —Henry David Thoreau

MAINTAIN AN OPEN MIND

There is no such thing on earth as an
uninteresting subject; the only thing that
can exist is an uninterested person.
                    —Gilbert Keith Chesterton

I have learned to use the word impossible
with the greatest caution.
                    —Wernher von Braun

If men could regard the events of their own
lives with more open minds they would
frequently discover that they did not really
desire the things they failed to obtain.
                    —André Maurois

Ugliness is a point of view; an ulcer is
wonderful to a pathologist.
                    —Austin O'Malley

The limits of the possible can only be
defined by going beyond them into the
impossible.
                    —Arthur C. Clarke

AVOID SELF-PITY

It has never been, and never will be easy
work! But the road that is built in hope is
more pleasant to the traveler than the road
built in despair, even though they both lead
to the same destination.
—Marion Zimmer Bradley

What poison is to food, self-pity is to life.
—Oliver C. Wilson

Pain is inevitable, suffering is optional.
—M. Kathleen Casey

Optimism and self-pity are the positive and
negative poles of modern cowardice.
—Cyril Connolly

Suffering isn't ennobling, recovery is.
—Christiaan N. Barnard

Opposition may become sweet to a man
when he has christened it persecution.
—George Eliot

MAKE THE BEST
OF A BAD SITUATION

Don't find fault, find a remedy.
—Henry Ford

Make good use of bad rubbish.
—Elizabeth Beresford

A clever person turns great troubles into little ones and little ones into none at all.
—Chinese proverb

A great wind is blowing, and that gives you either imagination or a headache.
—Catherine the Great

The cure for grief is motion.
—Elbert Hubbard

When written in Chinese, the word "crisis" is composed of two characters. One represents danger, and the other represents opportunity.
—John F. Kennedy

DON'T LET OTHERS
DEFINE WHO YOU ARE

Life would be a perpetual flea hunt if a man were obliged to run down all the innuendoes, inveracities, and insinuations and misrepresentations which are uttered against him.

—Henry Ward Beecher

He has great tranquillity of heart who cares neither for the praises nor the fault-finding of men.

—Thomas á Kempis

It's just like magic. When you live by yourself, all your annoying habits are gone!

—Merrill Markoe

Do not attempt to do a thing unless you are sure of yourself, but do not relinquish it simply because someone else is not sure of you.

—Stewart E. White

A POSITIVE ATTITUDE IS ITS OWN REWARD

I am seeking, I am striving, I am in it with all my heart.

—Vincent van Gogh

When we cannot get what we love, we must love what is within our reach.

—French proverb

A positive attitude may not solve all your problems, but it will annoy enough people to make it worth the effort.

—Herm Albright

It is our attitude at the beginning of a difficult task which, more than anything else, will affect its successful outcome.

—William James

The mind is its own place, and in itself can make a heaven of hell, a hell of heaven.

—John Milton

HAVE FAITH

Belief is a wise wager. Granted that faith cannot be proved, what harm will come to you if you gamble on its truth and it proves false? If you gain, you gain all; if you lose, you lose nothing.

—Blaise Pascal

How desperately we wish to maintain our trust in those we love! In the face of everything, we try to find reasons to trust. Because losing faith is worse than falling out of love.

—Sonia Johnson

The best and most beautiful things in the world cannot be seen or even touched— they must be felt with the heart.

—Helen Keller

There is no medicine like hope, no incentive so great, and no tonic so powerful as expectation of something tomorrow.

—O. S. Marden

Not truth, but faith it is that keeps the
world alive.
                    —Edna St. Vincent Millay

Great hopes make great men.
                    —Thomas Fuller

Hope is a very unruly emotion.
                    —Gloria Steinem

Not seeing is half-believing.
                    —Vita Sackville-West

Hope springs eternal in the human breast.
                    —Alexander Pope

Hope is a song in a weary throat.
                    —Pauli Murray

Hope—is not a feeling; it is something you do.
                    —Katherine Paterson

My reason nourishes my faith and my faith
my reason.
                    —Norman Cousins

Faith is much better than belief. Belief is when someone else does the thinking.
—R. Buckminster Fuller

More persons, on the whole, are humbugged by believing in nothing than by believing in too much.
—P. T. Barnum

Every time a child says, "I don't believe in fairies," there is a little fairy somewhere that falls down dead.
—Sir James M. Barrie

Sometimes I've believed as many as six possible things before breakfast.
—Lewis Caroll

TAKING RISKS

VIEW RISK AS
AN OPPORTUNITY FOR REWARD

Competition can damage self-esteem, create
anxiety, and lead to cheating and hurt
feelings. But so can romantic love.
—Mariah Burton Nelson

It is always the adventurers who do great
things, not the sovereigns of great empires.
—Charles De Montesquieu

I am willing to put myself through
anything; temporary pain or discomfort
means nothing to me as long as I can see
that the experience will take me to a new
level. I am interested in the unknown, and
the only path to the unknown is through
breaking barriers, an often painful process.
—Diana Nyad

Providence has hidden a charm in difficult
undertakings, which is appreciated only by
those who dare to grapple with them.
—Anne-Sophie Swetchine

Fortune favors the brave.

—Terence

Why not go out on a limb? Isn't that where the fruit is?

—Frank Scully

Grab a chance and you won't be sorry for a might have been.

—Arthur Mitchell Ransome

Love, like a chicken salad or restaurant hash, must be taken with blind faith or it loses its flavor.

—Helen Rowland

The men who have done big things are those who were not afraid to attempt big things, who were not afraid to risk failure in order to gain success.

—B. C. Forbes

All great reforms require one to dare a lot to win a little.

—William L. O'Neill

FAILURE ISN'T FATAL

Dare to be wrong, and to dream.
    —Friedrich von Schiller

If I had to live my life again, I'd make the same mistakes, only sooner.
    —Tallulah Bankhead

Even if my strength should fail, my daring will win me praise: in mighty enterprises even the will to succeed is enough.
    —Propertius

When in doubt, make a fool of yourself. There is a microscopically thin line between being brilliantly creative and acting like the most gigantic idiot on earth. So what the hell, leap.
    —Cynthia Heimel

'Tis better to have fought and lost than never to have fought at all.
    —Arthur Hugh Clough

YOU MUST TAKE RISKS TO
REALIZE YOUR POTENTIAL

During the first period of a man's life the
greatest danger is not to take the risk.
—Søren Kierkegaard

Most people live and die with their music
still unplayed. They never dare to try.
—Mary Kay Ash

Nothing ventured, nothing gained.
—Anon.

A ship in harbor is safe, but that is not what
ships are built for.
—John Shedd

Deliberation often loses a good chance.
—Latin proverb

Make voyages! Attempt them! There's
nothing else.
—Tennessee Williams

SIGNIFICANT CHANGE MAY REQUIRE SIGNIFICANT RISK

Caution has its place, no doubt, but we cannot refuse our support to a serious venture which challenges the whole of the personality. If we oppose it, we are trying to suppress what is best in man—his daring and his aspirations. And should we succeed, we should only have stood in the way of that invaluable experience which might have given a meaning to life.

—Carl Jung

I tore myself away from the safe comfort of certainties through my love for truth; and truth rewarded me.

—Sylvia Ashton Warner

Don't be afraid to take a big step if one is indicated. You can't cross a chasm in two small jumps.

—David Lloyd George

The only way to be absolutely safe is to never try anything for the first time.
—Magnus Pike

No one would have ever crossed the ocean if could have gotten off the ship in the storm.
—Charles F. Ketterling

The important thing is this: to be able at any moment to sacrifice what we are for what we would become.
—Charles Du Bos

Whenever you take a step forward, you are bound to disturb something.
—Indira Gandhi

To avoid an occasion for our virtues is a worse degree of failure than to push forward pluckily and make a fall.
—Robert Louis Stevenson

No guts, no glory.
—Anon.

WE FEEL MOST ALIVE
WHEN WE TAKE A CHANCE

We know what happens to people who stay
in the middle of the road. They get run over.
                              —Ambrose Bierce

I'm in love with the potential of miracles.
For me, the safest place is out on a limb.
                              —Shirley MacLaine

The chief danger in life is that you may
take too many precautions.
                              —Alfred Adler

It is so tempting to try the most difficult
thing possible.
                              —Jennie Jerome Churchill

To live without risk for me would be
tantamount to death.
                              —Jacqueline Cochran

Not Knowing, and Being Ready for Anything, Can Be a Strength

Lose yourself wholly; and the more you
lose, the more you will find.
                    —St. Catherine of Siena

Heroes take journeys, confront dragons,
and discover the treasure of their true selves.
                    —Carol Pearson

All growth is a leap in the dark, a
spontaneous, unpremeditated act without
benefit of experience.
                    —Henry Miller

We stand today on the edge of a new frontier.
                    —John F. Kennedy

Into the darkness they go, the wise and the
lovely.
                    —Edna St. Vincent Millay

STAYING FOCUSED ON YOUR GOALS

YOU MUST DREAM YOUR DREAM
BEFORE YOU CAN ACHIEVE IT

The future belongs to those who believe in
the beauty of the dream.
—Eleanor Roosevelt

If I had one wish for my children, it would
be that each of them would reach for goals
that have meaning for them as individuals.
—Lillian Carter

The man who has no imagination has no
wings.
—Muhammad Ali

Every woman dreams of her own political
career and her own place in life.
—Raisa M. Gorbachev

Instead of thinking about where you are,
think about where you want to be. It takes
twenty years of hard work to become an
overnight success.
—Diana Rankin

A person only grows so much as his horizon allows.

—John Powell

What is now proved was only once imagined.

—William Blake

Aim at nothing and you'll succeed.

—Anon.

A rock pile ceases to be a rock pile the moment a single man contemplates it, bearing within him the image of a cathedral.

—Antoine de Saint-Exupéry

It may be that those who do most, dream most.

—Stephen Leacock

All the works of man have their origin in creative fantasy. What right have we then to depreciate imagination.

—Carl Jung

WORK TOWARD YOUR GOAL EVERY DAY

Do the duty which lies nearest to you, the second duty will then become clearer.
—Thomas Carlyle

Until I die, I'm going to keep doing. My people need me. They need somebody that's not taking from them and is giving them something.
—Clara McBride Hale

To tend, unfailingly, unflinchingly, towards a goal, is the secret of success.
—Anna Pavlova

When you have a great and difficult task, something perhaps almost impossible, if you only work a little at a time, every day a little, suddenly the work will finish itself.
—Isak Dinesen

If you only keep adding little by little, it will soon become a big heap.
—Hesiod

DREAMS REQUIRE DISCIPLINE

Those who set their minds on virtue will do no evil.
                                    —Chinese proverb

Temptations come, as a general rule, when they are sought.
                                    —Margaret Oliphant

Great is the height I must scale, but the prospect of glory gives me strength.
                                    —Propertius

When things are steep, remember to stay level-headed.
                                    —Horace

Give to the world the best you have and the best will come back to you.
                                    —Madeline Bridges

It is not by spectacular achievements that man can be transformed, but by will.
                                    —Henrik Ibsen

BELIEVE IN ALL OF YOUR POSSIBILITIES

You can have anything you want if you want it desperately enough. You must want it with an inner exuberance that erupts through the skin and joins the energy that created the world.

—Sheila Graham

Our aspirations are our possibilities.

—Robert Browning

Let each become all he was created capable of becoming.

—Thomas Carlyle

I don't know much about being a millionaire, but I'll bet I'd be darling at it.

—Dorothy Parker

You will become as small as your controlling desire; as great as your dominant aspiration.

—James Allen

VISUALIZE YOUR DESTINATION CLEARLY

I never hit a shot, not even in practice,
without having a very sharp, in-focus
picture of it in my head.
—Jack Nicklaus

Ideals are like the stars: we never reach
them, but like the mariners of the sea, we
chart our course by them.
—Carl Schurz

If a man does not know what port he is
steering for, no wind is favorable to him.
—Seneca

Don't leave before the miracle happens!
—Anon.

Living in the past is a dull and lonely
business; looking back strains the neck
muscles, causes you to bump into people
not going your way.
—Edna Ferber

RESPECTING OTHERS

RECOGNIZE AND RESPECT DIFFERENCES

It is well, when judging a friend, to
remember that he is judging you with the
same godlike and superior impartiality.
                          —Arnold Bennett

There are no little events in life, those we
think of no consequence may be full of fate,
and it is at our own risk if we neglect the
acquaintances and opportunities that seem
to be casually offered, and of small
importance.
                              —Amelia Barr

Our loyalties must transcend our race, our
tribe, our class, and our nation; and this
means we must develop a world perspective.
                    —Martin Luther King, Jr.

Nothing is ever lost by courtesy. It is the
cheapest of pleasures, costs nothing, and
conveys much. It pleases him who gives and
receives and thus ... is twice blessed.
                          —Erastus Wiman

LOOK FOR THE GOOD IN OTHERS

It is a fine thing to have ability, but the ability to discover ability in others is the true test.

—Elbert Hubbard

Invest in the human soul. Who knows, it might be a diamond in the rough.

—Mary McLeod Bethune

Unless you bear with the faults of others, you betray your own.

—Publilius Syrus

Good is not good where better is expected.

—Thomas Fuller

A hero is someone we can admire without apology.

—Kitty Kelley

Wicked people are always surprised to find ability in those that are good.

—Marquis de Vauvenargues

KNOW WHEN TO SPEAK, WHEN TO LISTEN

Listening, not imitation, may be the sincerest form of flattery.
> —Dr. Joyce Brothers

Tact is after all a kind of mind-reading.
> —Sarah Orne Jewett

Advice is seldom welcome; and those who want it the most always like it the least.
> —Philip Dormer Stanhope,
> Earl of Chesterfield

Never fail to know that if you are doing all the talking, you are boring somebody.
> —Helen Gurley Brown

It's easier to be a critic than an author.
> —Yiddish proverb

Generosity gives assistance, rather than advice.
> —Marquis de Vauvenargues

CONSIDER YOURSELF ON
EQUAL FOOTING WITH OTHERS

If we had no faults of our own, we would
not take so much pleasure in noticing those
of others.
> —François de La Rochefoucauld

You can stand tall without standing on
someone. You can be a victor without
having victims.
> —Harriet Woods

To find a fault is easy; to do better may be
difficult.
> —Plutarch

The desire to conquer is itself a sort of
subjection.
> —George Eliot

The wise person questions himself, the fool
others.
> —Henri Arnold

BE PATIENT WITH OTHERS—AND YOURSELF

He who mistrusts most should be trusted least.
> —Theognis

Knowledge can be communicated but not wisdom.
> —Herman Hesse

Who thinks it just to be judged by a single error?
> —Beryl Markham

When your teenagers lose their temper with you, they are actually giving you a *gift*. They know that if they acted this way with a peer, that peer might abandon them. When they lose their temper with a parent, what they are really saying is, "I trust you. I know you'll never leave me."
> —Rebecca Fjelland Davis

Every man takes the limits of his own field of vision for the limits of the world.
> —Arthur Schopenhauer

Be Kind in All Encounters

I can live for two months on a good
compliment.
—Mark Twain

To be able to practice five things
everywhere under heaven constitutes perfect
virtue … gravity, generosity of soul,
sincerity, earnestness, and kindness.
—Confucius

It is terrible to destroy a person's picture of
himself in the interests of truth or some
other abstraction.
—Doris Lessing

Charm is the quality in others that makes
us more satisfied with ourselves.
—Henri Frédéric Amiel

Be nice to people on your way up because
you'll meet them on your way down.
—Wilson Mizner

SEIZING OPPORTUNITIES

POSITIVE CHANGE BEGINS WITH ONE SMALL STEP

All you have to do is look straight and see the road, and when you see it, don't sit looking at it—walk.

—Ayn Rand

Many things which cannot be overcome when they are together, yield themselves up when taken little by little.

—Plutarch

To choose is also to begin.

—Starhawk

Procrastination usually results in sorrowful regret. Today's duties put off until tomorrow give us a double burden to bear; the best way is to do them in their proper time.

—Ida Scott Taylor

I am prepared to go anywhere, provided it be forward.

—David Livingstone

You Can Make Your Own Breaks

To wait for someone else, or to expect
someone else to make my life richer, or
fuller, or more satisfying, puts me in a
constant state of suspension.
> —Kathleen Tierney Andrus

A wise man will make more opportunities
than he finds.
> —Sir Francis Bacon

Luck is a matter of preparation meeting
opportunity.
> —Oprah Winfrey

Luck is being ready for the chance.
> —James Frank Dobie

Do It Now

In any moment of decision the best thing you can do is the right thing, the next best thing is the wrong thing, and the worst thing you can do is nothing.

—Theodore Roosevelt

You don't need endless time and perfect conditions. Do it now. Do it today. Do it for twenty minutes and watch your heart start beating.

—Barbara Sher

We are given one life, and the decision is ours whether to wait for circumstances to make up our mind, or whether to act, and in acting, to live.

—Omar Nelson Bradley

Analysis kills spontaneity. The grain once ground into flour springs and germinates no more.

—Henri Frederic Amiel

DON'T WAIT—
TOMORROW MAY BE TOO LATE

Even if the doctor does not give you a year
... make one brave push and see what can
be accomplished in a week.
—Robert Louis Stevenson

You cannot do a kindness too soon, for you
never know how soon it will be too late.
—Ralph Waldo Emerson

I realize that if I wait until I am no longer
afraid to act, write, speak, be, I'll be sending
messages on a ouija board, cryptic
complaints from the other side.
—Audre Lorde

Yesterday is ashes; tomorrow wood. Only
today does the fire burn brightly.
—Eskimo proverb

It is better to waste one's youth than to do
nothing with it at all.
—Georges Courteline

Be Aware, Pay Attention, and Always Look for Opportunities

The gods cannot help those who do not seize opportunities.

—Chinese proverb

Nine-tenths of wisdom consists in being wise in time.

—Theodore Roosevelt

Look for opportunity. You can't wait for it to knock on the door.… You might not be home.

—Jinger Heath

Luck is largely a matter of paying attention.
—Susan M. Dodd

Great opportunities come to all, but many do not know they have met them. The only preparation to take advantage of them is simple fidelity to watch what each day brings.

—Albert E. Dunning

BE OPEN TO ALL POSSIBILITIES

Our duty, as men and women, is to proceed
as if limits to our ability did not exist. We
are collaborators in creation.
> —Pierre Teilhard de Chardin

Remember that to change your mind and
follow him who sets you right is to be none
the less free than you were before.
> —Marcus Aurelius

Consistency requires you to be as ignorant
today as you were a year ago.
> —Bernard Berenson

Consistency is the last refuge of the
unimaginative.
> —Oscar Wilde

What we need is not the will to believe, but
the wish to find out.
> —Bertrand Russell

YOU ARE LIMITED
ONLY BY YOUR DREAMS

To accomplish great things, we must not only act, but also dream; not only plan, but also believe.

—Anatole France

Dream lofty dreams, and as you dream, so shall you become. Your vision is the promise of what you shall one day be; your ideal is the prophecy of what you shall at last unveil.

—James Allen

The moment of enlightenment is when a person's dreams of possibilities become images of probabilities.

—Vic Braden

A genius is one who shoots at something no one else can see and hits it.

—Anon.

Dreams do come true, if we only wish hard enough.
—Sir James M. Barrie

We grow great by dreams.
—Woodrow Wilson

Nothing happens unless at first a dream.
—Carl Sandburg

A man is not old until regrets take the place of dreams.
—John Barrymore

Dream lofty dreams, and as you dream, so shall you become. Your vision is the promise of what you shall at last unveil.
—John Ruskin

WORKING HARD

HARD WORK IS THE BASIS OF EVERY GREAT ACHIEVEMENT

Genius is one percent inspiration and ninety-nine percent perspiration.
—Thomas Alva Edison

If your dream is a big dream, and if you want your life to work on the high level that you say you do, there's no way around doing the work it takes to get you there.
—Joyce Chapman

Hard work has made it easy. That is my secret. That is why I win.
—Nadia Comaneci

Big shots are only little shots who keep shooting.
—Christopher Morley

HARD WORK IS ITS OWN REWARD

Life well spent is long.
> —Leonardo da Vinci

Work! Thank God for the swing of it, for the clamoring, hammering, ring of it.
> —Anon.

Work banishes those three great evils: boredom, vice, and poverty.
> —Voltaire

The reward of a thing well done is to have done it.
> —Ralph Waldo Emerson

When you're following your energy and doing what you want all the time, the distinction between work and play dissolves.
> —Shakti Gawain

WORK WITH ALL THE COURAGE OF YOUR CONVICTIONS

If you aren't fired with enthusiasm, you will be fired with enthusiasm.
                                    —Vince Lombardi

The happiest excitement in life is to be convinced that one is fighting for all one is worth on behalf of some clearly seen and deeply felt good.
                                    —Ruth Benedict

Even if I knew that tomorrow the world would go to pieces, I would still plant my apple tree.
                                    —Martin Luther

A faint endeavor ends in a sure defeat.
                                    —Hannah Moore

Never let a day pass that you will have cause to say, I will do better tomorrow.
                                    —Brigham Young

You Inspire Others by Your Example

To know what people really think, pay regard to what they do, rather than what they say.
　　　　　　　　　　　　—Rene Descartes

Busy people are never busybodies.
　　　　　　　　　　　　—Ethel Watts Mumford

Nothing arouses ambition so much as the trumpet clang of another's fame.
　　　　　　　　　　　　—Baltasar Gracian

It's true that heroes are inspiring, but mustn't they also do some rescuing if they are to be worthy of their name? Would Wonder Woman matter if she only sent commiserating telegrams to the distressed?
　　　　　　　　　　　　—Jeanette Winterson

IF YOU'RE LUCKY ENOUGH TO HAVE A GIFT, MAKE THE MOST OF IT

There is no such thing as a great talent
without great will-power.

—Honoré de Balzac

I was born lucky, and I have lived lucky.
What I had was used. What I still have is
being used. Lucky.

—Katharine Hepburn

Men of genius do not excel in any
profession because they labor in it, but they
labor in it because they excel.

—William Hazlitt

The luck of having talent is not enough;
one must also have a talent for luck.

—Louis Hector Berlioz

It is one thing to be gifted and quite another
thing to be worthy of one's own gift.

—Nadia Boulanger

WISHING WON'T MAKE IT SO— TAKE ACTION IF YOU WANT RESULTS

What we have to learn to do, we learn by doing.

—Aristotle

You can't wait for inspiration. You have to go after it with a club.

—Jack London

Foolish indeed are those who trust to fortune.

—Lady Murasaki

I couldn't wait for success, so I went ahead without it.

—Jonathan Winters

No farmer ever plowed a field by turning it over in his mind.

—George E. Woodbury

If your ship doesn't come in, swim out to it!

—Jonathan Winters

MAKE YOUR OWN BREAKS

I know of no more encouraging fact than
the unquestionable ability of man to elevate
his life by conscious endeavor.
—Henry David Thoreau

You have to take it as it happens, but you
should try to make it happen the way you
want to take it.
—German proverb

You are no more exempt from time's
inexorable passing than Macbeth. Whether
time is your friend or foe depends on how
you use it
—Patricia Fripp

Those that are afraid of bad luck will never
know good.
—Russian proverb

The woman who can create her own job is
the one who will win fame and fortune.
—Amelia Earhart

THINGS WORTH HAVING ARE
WORTH FIGHTING FOR

It is easier to demolish a house than to
build one.

—Irish proverb

All effort is in the last analysis sustained by
faith that it is worth making.

—Ordway Tead

Excellence in any pursuit is the late, ripe
fruit of toil.

—W. M. L. Jay

That which we obtain too easily, we esteem
too lightly.

—Thomas Paine

What we want is never simple.

—Linda Pastan

Stay up and really burn the midnight oil.
There are no compromises.

—Leontyne Price

Don't Quit Until the Task is Finished

A winner never quits, and a quitter never wins.

—Anon.

Plough deep while sluggards sleep, and you shall have corn to sell and to keep.

—Benjamin Franklin

The great majority of men are bundles of beginnings.

—Ralph Waldo Emerson

Live with no time out.

—Simone de Beauvoir

I've got something inside of me, peasantlike and stubborn, and I'm in it till the end of the race.

—Truman Capote

Get a good idea and stay with it. Dog it, and work at it until it's done, and done right.

—Walt Disney

FAILURE IS NOT AN OPTION

I never quit trying. I never felt that I didn't
have a chance to win.
> —Arnold Palmer

The block of granite which was an obstacle
in the pathway of the weak becomes a
stepping-stone in the pathway of the strong.
> —Thomas Carlyle

Hold your head high, stick your chest out.
You can make it. It gets dark sometimes but
morning comes… Keep hope alive.
> —Jesse Jackson

They fail, and they alone, who have not
striven.
> —Thomas Aldrich

It's not worthy of human beings to give up.
> —Alva Reimer Myrdal

Persistence Pays When All Else Fails

Persistence is the master virtue. Without it,
there is no other.
                                    —Anon.

Genius at first is little more than a great
capacity for receiving discipline.
                                    —George Eliot

The race is not always to the swift, but to
those who keep on running.
                                    —Anon.

If the cat sits long enough at the hole, it
will catch the mouse.
                                    —Irish proverb

Victory belongs to the most persevering.
                                    —Napoleon Bonaparte

No great thing is created suddenly.
                                    —Epictetus

KEEP YOUR MIND ON YOUR GOALS

The future is a great land.
                                          —Anon.

Whatever you do, do it with intelligence,
and keep the end in view.
                                —Thomas á Kempis

Trouble, like the hill ahead, straightens out
when you advance upon it.
                                —Marcelene Cox

If one could recover the uncompromising
spirit of one's youth, one's greatest indignation
would be for what one has become.
                                          —André Gide

Every great work, every big
accomplishment, has been brought into
manifestation through holding to the
vision, and often just before the big
achievement, comes apparent failure and
discouragement.
                          —Florence Scovel Shinn

LEARNING FROM MISTAKES

AVOID MAKING THE SAME MISTAKE TWICE

There is nothing wrong with making
mistakes. Just don't respond with encores.
—Anon.

There is no reason to repeat bad history.
—Eleanor Holmes Norton

Do not be afraid of mistakes, providing you
do not make the same one twice.
—Eleanor Roosevelt

Those who cannot remember the past are
destined to repeat it.
—George Santayana

I try to extract something positive from
[every] situation, even if it's just learning
not to make the same mistake twice.
—Claudia Schiffer

Everyone Makes Mistakes— They're a Fact of Life

Those who never retract their opinions love themselves more than they love the truth.
                    —Joseph Joubert

Life is not life unless you make mistakes.
                    —Joan Collins

Mistakes are part of the dues one pays for a full life.
                    —Sophia Loren

Ever tried. Ever failed. No matter. Try again. Fail again. Fail better.
                    —Samuel Beckett

Flops are a part of life's menu and I've never been a girl to miss out on any of the courses.
                    —Rosalind Russell

PROGRESS IS A MATTER
OF TRIAL AND ERROR

A series of failures may culminate in the
best possible result.

—Gisela Richter

To begin to think with purpose, is to enter
the ranks of those strong ones who only
recognize failure as one of the pathways to
attainment.

—James Allen

No honest work of man or woman "fails"; it
feeds the sum of all human action.

—Michelene Wandor

I am not discouraged, because every wrong
attempt discarded is another step forward.

—Thomas Edison

The error of the past is the success of the
future. A mistake is evidence that someone
tried to do something.

—Anon.

MISTAKES ARE
OPPORTUNITIES TO GROW

Trouble brings experience, and experience brings wisdom.

—Anon.

The ultimate result of shielding men from the effects of folly is to fill the world with fools.

—Herbert Spencer

The most important of my discoveries has been suggested to me by my failures.

—Sir Humphrey Davy

Good judgment comes from experience, and experience comes from poor judgment.

—Anon.

It is not easy, but you have to be willing to make mistakes. And the earlier you make those mistakes, the better.

—Jane Cahill Pfeiffer

FINDING AND SHOWING COURAGE

IF YOU BELIEVE THAT YOU ARE BRAVE, OTHERS WILL BELIEVE IT, TOO

One man with courage makes a majority.
—Andrew Jackson

There are some women who seem to be born without fear, just as there are people who are born without the ability to feel pain.… Providence appears to protect such women, maybe out of astonishment.
—Margaret Atwood

Any coward can fight a battle when he's sure of winning; but give me the man who has pluck to fight when he's sure of losing. That's my way, sir; and there are many victories worse than defeat.
—George Eliot

It is not necessarily the size of the dog in the fight—it's the size of the fight in the dog.
—Dwight D. Eisenhower

Your Courage Can Help
Others to Be Brave

What after all has maintained the human race
on this old globe, despite all the calamities of
nature and all the tragic failings of mankind,
if not the faith in new possibilities and the
courage to advocate them?

—Jane Addams

To know how to say what others only know
how to think is what makes men poets or
sages; and to dare to say what others only
dare to think makes men martyrs or
reformers—or both.

—Elizabeth Charles

Courage is what it takes to stand up and
speak; courage is also what it takes to sit
down and listen.

—Anon.

He led his regiment from behind. He found
it less exciting.

—W. S. Gilbert

A Little Fear Can Be a Good Thing

Courage is resistance to fear, mastery of
fear—not absence of fear.
> —Mark Twain

A good scare is worth more to a man than
good advice.
> —Edgar Watson Howe

I wanted to be scared again. I wanted to feel
unsure again. That's the only way I learn,
the only way I feel challenged.
> —Connie Chung

Fear is a kind of bell, or gong, which rings
the mind into quick life and avoidance
upon the approach of danger. It is the soul's
signal for rallying.
> —Henry Ward Beecher

Being scared can keep a man from getting
killed, and often makes a better fighter out
of him.
> —Louis L'Amour

DON'T ALLOW FEAR
OR UNCERTAINTY TO IMMOBILIZE YOU

Hope is the anchor of the soul, the stimulus to action, and the incentive to achievement.
—Anon.

Man arrives as a novice at each age of his life.
—Nicolas Collins

Patience has its limits. Take it too far, and it's cowardice.
—George Jackson

Never let the fear of striking out get in your way.
—Babe Ruth

How very little can be done under the spirit of fear.
—Florence Nightingale

One had to take some action against fear when once it laid hold of one.
—Rainier Maria Rilke

USE YOUR FEARS AND CHALLENGES
TO EXPAND YOUR MIND

Courage is very important. Like a muscle, it is strengthened by use.

—Ruth Gordon

I have lived my life according to this principle: If I'm afraid of it, then I must do it.

—Erica Jong

Fear is an instructor of great sagacity, and the herald of all revolutions.

—Ralph Waldo Emerson

Fear makes us feel our humanity.

—Benjamin Disraeli

A coward's fear can make a coward valiant.

—Thomas Fuller

There is nothing in the universe that I fear, but that I shall not know all my duty or fail to do it.

—Mary Lyon

BE YOURSELF

Life is a great big canvas, and you should throw all the paint on it you can.
—Danny Kaye

My imagination makes me human and makes me a fool; it gives me all the world and exiles me from it.
—Ursula K. Le Guin

Almost every man wastes part of his life in attempts to display qualities which he does not possess, and to gain applause which he cannot keep.
—Samuel Johnson

If you're strong enough, there are no precedents.
—F. Scott Fitzgerald

When you have decided what you believe, what you feel must be done, have the courage to stand alone and be counted.
—Eleanor Roosevelt

DON'T LET OTHERS DEFINE YOU

No matter how well you perform, there's always somebody of intelligent opinion who thinks it's lousy.
—Laurence Olivier

I've always tried to go a step past wherever people expected me to end up.
—Beverly Sills

The widening of woman's sphere is to improve her lot. Let us do it, and if the world scoff, let it scoff—if it sneer, let it sneer.
—Lucy Stone

Never explain. Your friends do not need it and your enemies will not believe it anyway.
—Elbert Hubbard

If someone says can't, that shows you what to do.
—John Cage

Let Your Values Be Your Guide

The needle of our conscience is as good a compass as any.

—Ruth Wolff

Nothing is easier than self-deceit. For what each man wishes, that he also believes to be true.

—Demosthenes

There is only one history of any importance, and it is the history of what you once believed in, and the history of what you came to believe in.

—Kay Boyle

Courage, the footstool of the Virtues, upon which they stand.

—Robert Louis Stevenson

The one thing that doesn't abide by majority rule is a person's conscience.

—Harper Lee

ADJUSTING TO CHANGE

CHANGE MUST HAVE PURPOSE
TO BE TRULY USEFUL

Growth for the sake of growth is the
ideology of the cancer cell.

—Edward Abbey

Life is change. Growth is optional. Choose
wisely.

—Karen Kaiser Clark

It is not best to swap horses while crossing
the river.

—Abraham Lincoln

Change is an easy panacea. It takes character
to stay in one place and by happy there.

—Elizabeth Clarke Dunn

To become different from what we are, we
must have some awareness of what we are.

—Eric Hoffer

FEAR OF CHANGE IS FEAR OF LIFE ITSELF

What is the most rigorous law of our being?
Growth. No smallest atom of our moral,
mental, or physical structure can stand still
a year. It grows—it must grow; nothing can
prevent it.

—Mark Twain

Life is a series of spontaneous changes. Do
not resist them—that only creates sorrow.
Let reality be reality. Let things flow
naturally forward in whatever way they like.

—Lao Tzu

It is not the strongest of the species that
survive, nor the most intelligent, but the
one most responsive to change.

—Charles Darwin

Not everything that is faced can be changed,
but nothing can be changed until it is faced.

—James Baldwin

FLEXIBILITY AND CHANGE ARE NECESSARY FOR GROWTH

Nothing should be permanent except struggle with the dark side within ourselves.
—Shirley MacLaine

To be interested in the changing seasons is a happier state of mind than to be hopelessly in love with spring.
—George Santayana

To exist is to change, to change is to mature, to mature is to go on creating oneself endlessly.
—Henri L. Bergson

Continuity gives us roots; change gives us branches, letting us stretch and grow and reach new heights.
—Pauline R. Kezer

Growth is the only evidence of life.
—John Henry Newman

WE CAN'T AVOID CHANGE

All is change; all yields its place and goes.
—Euripides

We change, whether we like it or not.
—Ralph Waldo Emerson

Someday change will be accepted as life itself.
—Shirley MacLaine

Observe constantly that all things take place
by change, and accustom thyself to consider
that the nature of the Universe loves nothing
so much as to change the things which are,
and to make new things like them.
—Marcus Aurelius

Let nothing disturb thee,
Let nothing affright thee,
All things are passing,
God changeth never.

—Teresa of Avila

GROWING FROM ADVERSITY

ADVERSITY CAN HELP YOU SUCCEED

A certain amount of opposition is a great help to a man. Kites rise against, not with the wind.

—Lewis Mumford

We only think when we are confronted with a problem.

—John Dewey

It is better to be a fool than to be dead.

—Robert Louis Stevenson

I have always been pushed by the negative. The apparent failure of a play sends me back to my typewriter that very night, before the reviews are out.

—Tennessee Williams

The best way out is always through.

—Robert Frost

Necessity is often the spur to genius.

—Honoré de Balzac

Through Adversity, We Learn How Strong We Can Be

Happiness is beneficial for the body but it is grief that develops the power of the mind.
—Marcel Proust

Times of great calamity and confusion have been productive for the greatest minds. The purest ore is produced from the hottest furnace. The brightest thunder-bolt is elicited from the darkest storm.
—Charles Caleb Colton

What does not destroy me, makes me stronger.
—Friedrich Wilhelm Nietzsche

Storms make the oak take deeper root.
—George Herbert

Difficulties strengthen the mind, as labor does the body.
—Seneca

BE THANKFUL FOR YOUR TRIALS
AND ALL THEY TEACH YOU

The difficulties which I meet with in order to realize my existence are precisely what awaken and mobilize my activities, my capacities.

—José Ortega Y Gasset

Every life has dark tracts and long stretches of somber tint, and no representation is true to fact which dips its pencil only in light, and flings no shadows on the canvas.

—Alexander MacLaren

Maybe one day we will be glad to remember even these hardships.

—Virgil

When a thing ceases to be a subject of controversy, it ceases to be a subject of interest.

—William Hazlitt

YOUR HEART AND SOUL ARE STRONGER THAN YOU KNOW

Be willing to access joy in the face of adversity.

—C. W. Metcalf

We must accept finite disappointment, but we must never lose infinite hope.

—Martin Luther King, Jr.

I think hearts are very much like glasses—if they do not break with the first ring, they usually last a considerable time.

—Letitia Landon

When you can't remember why you're hurt, that's when you're healed. When you have to work real hard to re-create the pain, and you can't quite get there, that's when you're better.

—Jane Fonda

A good cry lightens the heart.

—Yiddish proverb

Today's Adversity May Bring Tomorrow's Opportunity

Supporting myself at an early age was the best training for life I could have possibly received.

—Lea Thompson

If a door slams shut it means that God is pointing to an open door further on down.

—Anna Delaney Peale

Endure, and preserve yourself for better things.

—Virgil

Difficulties mastered are opportunities won.

—Winston Churchill

Accept the challenges, so you may feel the exhilaration of victory.

—General George S. Patton

Life begins on the other side of despair.

—Jean-Paul Sartre

Discontent is the first step in the progress
of a man or a nation.
—Oscar Wilde

Noble discontent is the path to heaven.
—Thomas Higginson

The apprenticeship of difficulty is one
which the greatest of men have had to serve.
—Samuel Smiles

HAVING VISION

Imagine, And Make
Your Dreams Reality

Vision is the art of seeing things invisible.
—Jonathan Swift

Make-believe colors the past with innocent distortion, and it swirls ahead of us in a thousand ways—in science, in politics, in every bold intention.
—Shirley Temple Black

The problems of the world cannot possibly be solved by skeptics or cynics whose horizons are limited by the obvious realities. We need men who can dream of things that never were.
—John F. Kennedy

There are those that look at things the way they are, and ask why. I dream of things that never were, and ask why not.
—Robert F. Kennedy

IF YOU HAVE VISION,
YOU WILL ALWAYS HAVE HOPE

Inside myself is a place where I live alone
and that's where you renew your springs
that never dry up.

—Pearl S. Buck

An idea is salvation by imagination.

—Frank Lloyd Wright

Our imagination is the only limit to what
we can hope to have in the future.

—Charles F. Kettering

The song that we hear with our ears is only
the song that is sung in our hearts.

—Ouida

Faith is the daring of the soul to go father
than it can see.

—William Newton Clark

When we can't dream any longer, we die.

—Emma Goldman

KEEP AN OPEN MIND
AND LET IDEAS FLOW FREELY

What a surprise to find you could shift the contents of your head like rearranging furniture in a room.

—Lisa Alther

Little girls are cute and small only to adults. To one another they are not cute. They are life-sized.

—Margaret Atwood

Genius means little more than the faculty of perceiving in an unhabitual way.

—William James

You can always trust information given you by people who are crazy; they have an access to truth not available through regular channels.

—Sheila Ballantyne

Your Vision May Impact Others

Your audience gives you everything you
need. They tell you. There is no director
who can direct you like an audience.
—Fanny Brice

We must not, in trying to think about how
we can make a big difference, ignore the
small daily differences we can make which,
over time, add up to big differences that we
often cannot foresee.
—Marian Wright Edelman

Never tell people how to do things. Tell
them what to do and they will surprise you
with their ingenuity.
—General George S. Patton

People who concentrate on giving good
service always get more personal satisfaction
as well as better business. How can we get
better service? One way is by trying to see
ourselves as others do.
—Patricia Fripp

THOSE WITH VISION ARE NOT LIMITED BY THEIR PHYSICAL BEING

One may have good eyes and yet see nothing.
—Italian proverb

Death is the last enemy: once we've got past that I think everything will be all right.
—Alice Thomas Ellis

No one was ever great without some portion of divine inspiration.
—Cicero

Children seldom have a proper sense of their own tragedy, discounting and keeping hidden the true horrors of their short lives, humbly imagining real calamity to be some prestigious drama of the grown-up world.
—Shirley Hazzard

You can't depend on your eyes when your imagination is out of focus.
—Mark Twain

NOT EVERYONE WILL AGREE
WITH YOUR VISION

The creative person is both more primitive and more cultivated, more destructive, a lot madder and a lot saner, than the average person.

—Frank Barron

Discovery consists of seeing what everyone has seen and thinking what nobody has thought.

—Albert Szent-Györgyi

There's an element of truth in every idea that lasts long enough to be called corny.

—Irving Berlin

The cleverly expressed opposite of any generally accepted idea is worth a fortune to somebody.

—F. Scott Fitzgerald

THE ABILITY TO HAVE VISION IS A GREAT GIFT

By learning to contact, listen to, and act on our intuition, we can directly connect to the higher power of the universe and allow it to become our guiding force.

—Shakti Gawain

Art is the signature of civilizations.

—Beverly Sills

Children see things very well sometimes— and idealists even better.

—Lorraine Hansbury

They who dream by day are cognizant of many things which escape those who dream only by night.

—Edgar Allan Poe

Freedom is always and exclusively freedom for the one who thinks differently.

—Rosa Luxemburg

ACT ON YOUR IDEAS
AND SEE THEM THROUGH

The insight to see possible new paths, the courage to try them, the judgment to measure results—these are the qualities of a leader.

—Mary Parker Follett

The engineering is secondary to the vision.

—Cynthia Ozick

There is one thing stronger than all the armies in the world, and that is an idea whose time has come.

—Victor Hugo

For a long time it seemed to me that real life was about to begin, but there was always some obstacle in the way. Something had to be got through first, some unfinished business; time still to be served, a debt to be paid. Then life would begin. At last it dawned on me that these obstacles were my life.

—Bette Howland

COMMIT FULLY TO YOUR
VISION AND ITS SUCCESS

Every production of genius must be the
production of enthusiasm.
—Benjamin Disraeli

First, have a definite, clear practical ideal; a
goal, an objective. Second, have the
necessary means to achieve your ends;
wisdom, money, materials, and methods.
Third, adjust all your means to that end.
—Aristotle

Vision. It reaches beyond the thing that is,
into the conception of what can be.
Imagination gives you the picture. Vision
gives you the impulse to make the picture
your own.
—Robert Collier

There is a boundary to men's passions when
they act from feelings; but none when they
are under the influence of imagination.
—Edmund Burke

The person with a fixed goal, a clear picture of his desire, or an ideal always before him, causes it, through repetition, to be buried deeply in his subconscious mind and is thus enabled, thanks to its generative and sustaining power, to realize his goal in a minimum of time and with a minimum of physical effort. Just pursue the thought unceasingly. Step by step you will achieve realization, for all your faculties and powers become directed to that end.

—Claude M. Bristol

If you deny yourself commitment, what can you do with your life?

—Harvey Fierstein

If you don't make a total commitment to whatever you're doing, then you start looking to bail out the first time the boat starts leaking. It's tough enough getting that boat to shore with everybody rowing, let alone when a guy stands up and starts putting his life jacket on.

—Lou Holz

SEARCH FOR THE TRUTH
WITHIN YOUR VISION

Illusion is the dust the devil throws in the eyes of the foolish.

—Minna Antrim

There's a period of life when we swallow a knowledge of ourselves and it becomes either good or sour inside.

—Pearl Bailey

I am certain of nothing but the holiness of the heart's affections, and the truth of imagination.

—John Keats

Truth is simply whatever you can bring yourself to believe.

—Alice Childress

There's folks 'ud stand on their heads and then say the fault was i' their boots.

—George Eliot